A Tiny Book of Joy

10 Ways to Bring More Joy and Creativity to Your Day – Every Day

Olya Kornienko

Copyright © 2023 by Olya Kornienko

All rights reserved.

No part of this publication may be reproduced, distributed or transmitted in any form or by any means, including photocopying, recording, or other electronic or mechanical methods, without the prior written permission of the publisher, except in the case of brief quotations embodied in critical reviews and certain other non-commercial uses permitted by copyright law. For permission requests, write to the author at: olya@olyakornienko.com

Author Name: Olya Kornienko

Publisher Name: Yellow Flower Media

Contact Information: www.olyakornienko.com

First Edition

ISBN: 978-0-6456748-2-8

This book is not intended to be a substitute for professional medical advice. Always seek the guidance of your doctor or other qualified health professional with any questions you may have regarding your health or a medical condition.

For my Mamochka.
For all the reasons.

Contents

Introduction ii

1. Defining Success 1
2. The Difference Between a Hobby, Job, Career & Vocation.............................. 9
3. Creating a Morning Ritual................... 15
4. Understanding What You Truly Want to Do in Your Life 20
5. Creating a Joy List 27
6. Letting Yourself Rest........................ 35
7. Getting to Know Yourself 40
8. Being Joyful During Difficult Times 45
9. Being Present with Mindfulness........... 51
10. Taking Care of Your Physical Health 55
Conclusion: A Letter to the Reader........... 60
Acknowledgements 63
Book Bonuses.................................... 67
A Note From the Author 68
About the Author 69
Reading List..................................... 71

Introduction

"You are Braver than you believe, Stronger than you seem, and Smarter than you think."
- Christopher Robin (by A.A. Milne)

After years of spending money on courses and memberships and trying to make my online businesses work, I felt empty and exhausted.

Even after I was finally making money while I slept with my online Pilates program, I didn't feel any more joyful or happy.

I knew I wanted to feel joyful and be doing the things I really wanted to do: writing, painting, and maybe making a movie. But I hadn't written anything besides my blog posts, and I hadn't opened my watercolours for over twenty years.

I'd often find myself thinking if I could just get [insert what I wanted at that moment], I would finally be allowed to feel joy, happiness or just good.

If only I could get slim and stay that way without constantly thinking about food or how much I exercise, then I could be happy and do the things I really wanted to. That wish actually came true, but it didn't make me feel how I hoped it would.

If I only could get into the film industry, then I'd feel so much more fulfilled and joyful. I worked on the Great Gatsby, Underbelly, Getaway, and a bunch of other projects and—you guessed it—I still didn't feel the way I wanted to feel. I met amazing people, felt exhilaration from seeing the final cut after countless hours of work, and had a rollercoaster of feelings in between. Sometimes it felt joyful, but something was constantly missing.

I would think of more things that must happen before I could feel joyful: no debt, a big house, work from wherever. The list kept growing.

Maybe you're at the same stage in your life. You feel like you no longer know what you want, you feel you do things for everyone other than yourself, and you don't feel happy. You don't feel joyful.

What if it's possible to feel joy sooner? Maybe even today and then every day afterwards? What if there is no secret and not only chosen people can access this feeling? What if it could be you?

It certainly can be you. As soon as you decide that you can be joyful today. As soon as you choose to do what you genuinely want to be doing and do it today.

So simple yet so complicated at the same time.

I finally started painting again, and it brought me so much joy. I'm writing this book for you, and it brings me joy. I try to make my home the place I'm currently in (even if I will leave it in a few months), and that brings me joy.

I hope that by the end of this book (hopefully a lot earlier), you'll realise that joy is accessible now. It's available to you right this moment. You can do what you want to do now, today, this week.

I wrote this book with three intentions for you, my reader. I want you to:

- Feel hope and certainty that you can experience joy now, despite your situation.

- Know that you can start writing, painting, and making that movie you've been dreaming about now, not when xyz happens.

- Follow the simple steps I provide and start practising your art. Do what you want to do every day.

You'll get tools and exercises that will help you start doing what you want to be doing, whatever it might be: dancing, writing poetry or a screenplay, creating a collage, or finally trying pottery.

I've created a workbook for you to go along with all the questions and exercises in each chapter. As you go through, write down answers and use it as a tool to figure out exactly what you want to be doing.

You can download your workbook here: https://olyakornienko.com/a-tiny-book-of-joy-bonuses.

CHAPTER ONE

Defining Success

"My goal is no longer to get more done, but rather to have less to do."
- Francine Jay

I was about five or six and outside playing when I saw them. Not a couple but a whole bunch of delicious fruit that was so exotic and rare that I only remember eating it once before. I could not believe that this man was carrying such a HUGE bunch of them.

I thought that fruit was the most delicious thing in the whole world. That fruit represented the wonderful world that was abroad, somewhere only special people could go. Somewhere where they could eat that fruit any day they wanted.

This was me growing up in Soviet Union's Estonia.

And those fruits were bananas.

I ran home and asked my mum to go to the shops and look for bananas. She said that they must have brought them from abroad, and there were no bananas in the shops.

I wanted to live abroad. I wanted to eat bananas every day. That was a luxury. I thought that if I could only move overseas, live in a foreign country, and speak another language other than my own Russian; I would feel I had achieved everything I wanted.

Having money and living in a beautiful house are a given if you live abroad. Or so the majority in the Soviet Union thought.

Then Estonia gained independence from the Soviet Union in 1991, and things started to change. I travelled overseas for the first time a year after I finished high school. Then, in 2001, I moved to Australia.

Finally, I could eat bananas every day. That was what success was, right?

I started thinking more about what success really means.

Did I feel successful because I achieved something that was pretty much impossible when I lived in the USSR? I lived in beautiful Australia and spoke English fluently. Yet, I didn't think of myself as successful.

I realised that I had achieved some of the things that I wanted. Besides eating bananas whenever I wanted, I worked in fashion, sewing samples of the most exquisite lingerie available in Australia, taught Pilates online and offline, produced a short film, and worked in some of the most desirable production offices for film & TV.

When I was a coach, one of my wonderful clients published multiple books. Another amazing young lady established a charity and ran organ donor awareness campaigns. Another client successfully re-entered a male-dominated industry after an extended break looking after her kids and won awards for her amazing work.

But here was that word again – success.

The more I looked at the success in my life and the success of the people around me, the more I noticed that success generally meant the achievement of some goal. It was something temporary rather than a state of being, and because it was only temporary, it felt like a never-ending achievement marathon.

I wanted something different. Something that could stay with me for longer. Something that was not so black or white. Something with more ease and grace.

I started to wonder, what if success wasn't just the achievement of a particular goal but something more consistent, more constant in my life?

Something that would ooze through the practice rather than the completion of the project.

Not a thirty-day meditation challenge, but a consistent five-minute practice every day. That would be a success. All of a sudden, success was more achievable than ever. When I started to focus on what was important to me rather than what social media told me was, my everyday mood lifted, and I began to have a more positive and uplifting experience.

What does success mean to you?

What success means for someone else does not have to be a measure of success for you. For some people, it's fame and an eight-figure business; for others, it's having time to travel or be with their families.

Shanna Skidmore, the creator of *The Blueprint Model*™, teaches four Core Motivators™ of success: creative expression, time, challenge, and impact.

If your core motivator is creative expression, creativity and making things that you love are what motivate and inspire you. You might make great money as a wedding photographer, but you won't be inspired if you don't do some creative projects.

If your core motivator is time, then having control over your schedule is the most important thing for you. You want to be able to dictate what hours you work and when you don't work.

When your core motivator is a challenge, you are motivated by goals. You may even start one project before you finish another one. You are always on the lookout for a new source of income, a new challenge, or a new project.

Finally, when you are motivated by impact, you want to give to a cause you believe in. For example, you may volunteer your services to the not-for-profit organisation you believe in once a year. This would inspire you to keep going.

At different stages of your business and life, you may have different motivators, but your core motivator will stay the same.

When I got introduced to the core motivators, I thought that my core motivator was time. I wanted to be my own boss and establish my working hours. But later, I realised that being creative and making beautiful things were even more important to me.

I wanted to make money so I had time to paint and write. Can you see what my motivator is? Creative expression.

As you'll find out in the next chapter, when I figured out the difference between a hobby, job, career, and vocation, I was able to confirm with

100% confidence that my core motivator is creative expression.

Even though right now my motivator is a challenge (to finish and publish this book), I know that painting and writing feed my soul, light me up, and help me with everything else in life.

Once you know your core motivator, you can define what success means to you. So, what would success look like for you? Is it working three days a week and spending the rest of your time with your family? Is it running an online empire or making art and having clients who want to buy what you create?

The best way to figure out your definition of success is to journal what your ideal life would look like. I used to feel frustrated when journalling about my ideal day and life. I tried to fit in all the different ideas I had, plus what I was already doing. In the end, I didn't feel inspired by this new picture, just exhausted.

This was back when I was building an online Pilates business and working in the production office. On top of that, I wanted to produce movies. My ideal day had so much in it (it was unrealistic, to say the least) that I didn't know how to do it all – produce, write, teach, and a thousand other things.

One day, I let myself dream and write without trying to cram in everything I was already working on at the time. Then I re-read it. There wasn't a single word about Pilates. Deep down, I knew that I didn't want to teach Pilates anymore. Even though I'd heard so many times how what I taught helped people, I knew that it was not what I was meant to be doing or what I wanted to be doing. That was my first step into a more joyful life.

Taking all this in, set a timer for 15 minutes and answer these questions:

- In an ideal world, how would you spend your days?

- What do you do?

- How many days do you work per week?

- How much time do you work and rest?

- What do you do when you don't work?

- Who are you spending your days with?

- What do you do in the morning, during the day, and in the evening?

- How do you feel?

- If you didn't have to worry about money or taking care of anyone else, what would your life look like?

Sometimes it's hard to start imagining a different kind of life, or maybe you feel like you've done this exercise a million times. If so, start with how you want to feel.

Now, you can answer the most important question: What does success mean to you?

Take some time and journal. If you haven't already, download your beautiful workbook where there is space to write: https://olyakornienko.com/a-tiny-book-of-joy-bonuses.

I realised that success for me is about having time with people I love and having time for creativity. I want to be able to write and paint whatever and whenever I choose to.

If you are still confused, have too much to fit into your ideal day, or feel like you want to do it all and need a minimum of five lives to get it all done, then the next chapter will help give you a solution.

CHAPTER TWO

The Difference Between a Hobby, Job, Career & Vocation

"Follow what feels good in the moment, every moment, and it will lead you through a most excellent life."
- Jen Sincero

Chances are, you enjoy doing a lot of things, and you hear from every corner of the internet that you should make money doing what you love. While this is a great concept, it doesn't mean that you have to make money out of everything you enjoy doing.

I used to try making money from everything I enjoyed doing. I created businesses so that I could earn money doing what I enjoyed more than my day job, and I bought every possible domain name for every business idea that came to my mind.

But creating a business to make money so you can finally do what you want to be doing later doesn't work. Those businesses may bring in money, but you'll be exhausted when you get there. There's also a real chance you won't make money and will just feel defeated.

For years I bought courses and tried making money with anything I thought could make money: cupcakes, cotton tops (what I really wanted to do was silk knickers, but who would buy them, I thought), online Pilates courses, video marketing consulting, the list went on.

How could I possibly make money painting if I hadn't painted in twenty years?! Or make money as a scriptwriter if I had never written a script? I went through multiple jobs because I couldn't make money with what I thought I would enjoy more. Eventually, I ended up back doing bookkeeping. After all, for years it was a job that paid me money.

Two things changed my mind about trying to make money doing what I love. The first was reading Steal Like an Artist by Austin Kleon. He wrote, "We used to have hobbies; now we have 'side hustles.'"

Just because everyone enjoys your baked blueberry cheesecake doesn't mean you have to open a bakery. Just because you love painting doesn't mean you have to open an art gallery. And just because you're interested in fashion or enjoy making dresses doesn't mean you have to start a fashion label.

Leave something for yourself that can just be your hobby, something that you do purely because you enjoy it without expecting a profit.

Isn't it liberating and yet scary to start doing something you simply enjoy doing? Scandalous, isn't it? Doing something for fun. In our busy world, it seems like an impossible luxury.

Yet, it can be your reality.

The second thing that drastically changed my mind about making money doing what I love was stumbling across an extract from Elizabeth Gilbert's course, where she distinguishes between hobbies, jobs, careers, and vocations.

If you haven't already, watch her video on YouTube: Elizabeth Gilbert on Distinguishing Between Hobbies, Jobs, Careers, & Vocation | Acumen Academy.

She explains that jobs are something that we obtain to make money. We're adults, and we're supposed to take care of ourselves financially. You may also have to take care of the people dependent on you. You might enjoy doing what you do for a job, or not. If you hate your job then, of course, it's best to find another one.

A career is something that you dedicate the majority of your time to; you're willing to work more than normal hours. You don't want to have a career that you hate, and you don't have to have a career.

Then you have a vocation. It's a calling. A vocation is something you love doing so much that you cannot live without it. Maybe you could, but you would feel depleted and restrained, like something was missing from your life. If you feel this way, it's because you're trying to refuse yourself something you love doing.

I felt this way for years when I refused the pleasure of painting. Painting was something I had always done since I was a child up until the age of twenty. But after I didn't get into Art University and moved to Australia, I stopped painting. I did a few scribbles in pencil and a couple of collages but years went by before I finally opened my watercolours, dipped my brush, and began to paint.

Elizabeth Gilbert's vocation is writing. She would write no matter what. But she did everything she could to not put pressure on her writing to make money. She waited tables for quite a while, even when her first books were published.

If you get good at your vocation, with some luck, your vocation may become your job (you'll make money doing what you love) and then it could become your career.

Writing was something I enjoyed doing as a teenager and in high school. After I started studying at the university, my creative writing changed to research and academic writing and again, I let go of something I enjoyed very much. Perhaps this is another vocation for me – who says I can't have two? I don't expect both writing and painting to become my career. In fact, I don't want to put any pressure on my painting to make money, even though it would be fabulous to sell a painting.

A hobby is something that you enjoy doing without any monetary reward: making aeroplane models, building Lego castles, or knitting scarves. You don't have to have a hobby, just like you don't have to have a career.

Elizabeth Gilbert's words finally made me want to do bookkeeping and feel pretty good about it. I am good at bookkeeping, it's easy for me, and I have an amazing client I love working with. Plus, I am paid well. I click some buttons, chase invoices, and then I can paint and write when I finish my job. Sounds like a great arrangement to me.

Don't delay your happiness, and don't delay doing what you enjoy doing because you can't make money with it. When you do something you enjoy, things start to shift, and maybe, one day, you'll be opening your exhibition and placing a "sold" sticker next to your work. Maybe, one day, you'll see your name in the opening credits on a big screen.

"You can make money and do what you love" is a much more joyful motto to live by than *"Make money doing what you love"*.

Your Turn

In your workbook or in your journal, answer the following questions:

- What would be your vocation?
- What job would you be good at?
- What kind of career would you love to have (if you want one)?
- What can be your hobby?

Next, let's look at how you can start living your dream life today rather than leaving it to some uncertain future.

CHAPTER THREE

Creating a Morning Ritual

"Let the beauty of what you love be what you do."
- Rumi

When I was working on the Great Gatsby, I'd pass a café every morning on my walk to Fox Studios. Every morning, I saw a man reading a newspaper with an espresso sitting in front of him. I'd watch him sip his coffee, reading peacefully before (as I found out later) he started his shift as a nurse in the nearby hospital.

I decided that I wanted to create a morning ritual as he had.

I didn't know much about rituals, and YouTube wasn't yet overflowing with all kinds of content on them. But all I wanted was to have that consistency and peace I saw in the man with his espresso and newspaper. So, I decided that my morning ritual would consist of lemon water and exercise. I later added mediation, morning pages (which we'll talk about later) and a walk when I can.

At one stage, after watching some of the videos on morning routines, I overloaded my morning, and it became too much. Instead of feeling energised, I felt overwhelmed and disappointed because I couldn't complete everything on my list. Don't make the same mistake.

Look over your answers in the first chapter, where you explored what you would like to do on your ideal average day. Now, focus only on what you would do in the morning on that day.

Ideally, you might need to have more time for everything on your list, but you can still start doing what you want to be doing in the morning now. Maybe it's a coffee with an article from your favourite blogger and a walk in nature. Or maybe you'd like to be up before everyone else, have your tea in your favourite cup, meditate, do some yoga, journal, slowly get ready, and have a healthy breakfast followed by a walk to the beach.

In the workbook that you downloaded from the bonus section or in your journal, list some things you'd like to experience before starting your day. At this point, don't focus on the length of each experience. You may want to have an hour of yoga and half an hour of meditation, but if you have never done this before or only have an hour free in the morning, you'll only get frustrated and give up on the practice.

What you see in morning ritual videos might not be what you feel like doing for your morning. Think about what will energise you. It doesn't need to be coffee – maybe a glass of lemon water is on your list. What will bring you the feeling you want to feel on your ideal morning?

Now, look at how much time you have before you get out of the door for work or if you work from home before you sit down in your workspace and start working.

If you're limited on time, especially if you have kids who tend to get up very early, look at how much time you have for yourself before you need to attend to everyone else's needs and wants. Could you start waking up ten minutes earlier? It may not seem like a lot, but it's ten minutes that you can use to start your day slowly, and it may be the way you want to start your ideal morning. Ten minutes is all you need for a stretch, short yoga practice, or meditation.

When I used to teach Pilates, I always gave an example of doing just ten squats or ten minutes of exercise per day. If you do that, five days per week, that's 50 minutes per week and 2,600 minutes per year; 2,600 minutes is 43.33 hours.

Do you think you would make some progress if you exercised for 43 hours? This example works well for learning a foreign language, too.

Once you establish how much time you have and what you would like to include in your morning ritual, look at how many minutes you can dedicate to each experience on your list. Remember that you need to include around two to five minutes to switch between activities.

The next step is to simplify. How can you simplify your morning ritual so it feels pleasant instead of a go-go list?

The final step is to try your morning ritual. Don't get up more than ten minutes earlier than you normally would. Start gradually. If you can't fit all the items on your list in your morning, don't. Start with what you can. Then you'll be able to get up ten minutes earlier the next week and add something else in.

You may want to switch things around and move your workout to the evening if you find you prefer exercising in the evening. I know that I must exercise in the morning because it feels great, even if I sometimes need to make myself exercise, and I'm not the type of person who can exercise in the afternoon. In fact, there's a 99.5% chance that I won't.

Gradually, you'll come up with a morning ritual that is exactly what you want. One of the most important things to remember when you start doing something new is don't beat yourself up if you miss a day. Do it the next day. When you get unwell, things will need to be adjusted, and that's ok. Do your best. It's about doing it rather than trying to get it done perfectly.

Starting your day with an ideal morning creates motion that will propel your life in the direction you dream about. If you're finding it difficult to understand what you want in your dream life, the next chapter will give you some questions to help you find the answers.

CHAPTER FOUR

Understanding What You Truly Want to Do in Your Life

"What is it you plan to do with your one wild and precious life?"
- Mary Oliver

Maybe you've known what you wanted to do since you were a toddler. But maybe you're like me and wanted to do so many things that you never really knew how to answer the question, what do you want to be when you grow up?

From a dressmaker (like my auntie) to working with dolphins (because my friend wanted to), to archaeology, orthopedic surgery, fashion and interior design, art, teaching English, acting and producing, I couldn't figure out what I wanted to do.

When people ask about what we want to do with our lives, we focus on money-making activities. Hence, why we get trapped trying to figure out how we can make money from what we love doing.

When I learned about online marketing in 2008 and the possibility of making money literally out of anything, I couldn't stop buying domain names for various ideas and started half a dozen websites.

I used to say, "I don't know what I want to do", meaning what kind of job I wanted. As a result of repeating that same phrase, I continued not knowing; I repeated it so many times in my mind that I was 100% sure that I didn't know what I wanted to do. I was so focused on making money in a more pleasant way than bookkeeping, which I disliked.

If we tell ourselves something all the time, it becomes our truth (our belief), and the only way out is to learn a different truth. I found a great alternative phrase in one of Jen Sincero's books: *"Answers are everywhere."*

Marie Forleo, a brilliant entrepreneur and founder of B-School, offers another: *"Everything is figureoutable."*

I started repeating them both. Marie suggests saying these words while you do something physical because it helps engrave them into your brain. I do squats while I repeat, "Everything is figureoutable." Good for the mind and good for the body!

Then you need to listen to any little ideas and curiosities within yourself. It doesn't matter if it doesn't make sense or seems silly. If you don't know what you want to be doing, why don't you try what you are half curious about?

Start exploring where your curiosity and interest take you. This will energise you and give you so much joy. When you feel happier, when you feel more joyful, you behave differently, you feel differently, and beautiful things can happen.

In Mel Robbins' two-minute video, Don't Know What You Want? Answer This Question, she says that you certainly know what you want, but you've told yourself that you're too old or you can't make money from it.

Isn't that brilliant?! It's so true. When I came up with any ideas, I thought it was too late for me or I had no idea how to make money out of what I thought I wanted to do.

If you still doubt what you want to be doing, then this simple exercise is for you: Look back over what you wrote about your ideal average day. What did you write about? What did you do on your ideal day and week?

If you allow yourself to dream and design your ideal average day without trying to adjust it to your current circumstances, it will show you exactly what you want to be doing.

So many times, I've written, "I want to work three days a week so that I can write and paint on Thursday and Friday." Why can't I write and paint all five days then? Isn't that what I want to be doing?

But remember what we talked about in the chapter on the difference between a job, hobby, career, and vocation. You don't have to make money out of everything you enjoy doing. And you don't have to wait to get a certain amount of money to start doing what you enjoy.

I refused the joy of painting for over two decades. I thought that when I finally made my online business work, then I'd have time and permission to paint. All while trying to make a business work that I had no real interest in.

Once you know what you want to experience or what you want to be doing, you can start doing it. You don't have to quit your job, sell all your possessions, and move to Bali to write your script. You can start writing for 15 minutes every morning this week. You can sign up for a couple of singing lessons today if you decide that you'd like to go back to your idea of being on stage and singing in front of people.

Take some action. Thinking about it and journaling about it is good, but nothing compares with taking some steps. You might do a course in fashion, enjoy it, and complete it, but then decide that it's not for you, even if you've worked in fashion before and have wanted to be in fashion since high school. This happened to me, and you may have a similar story to share.

Maybe you're not taking any action steps because you want a guarantee that it will work. And it's true that taking steps does not guarantee results. Why would you throw your energy, your time, and all your resources into something that you don't have a guarantee will work?

Trust me, I get you. About a decade ago, I was sitting in one of the Great Gatsby's production offices with Barrie Osborne, who'd agreed to have a chat with me. I was so excited. My pen and notebook were ready. I thought he would give me all the answers and step-by-step instructions on how to become a great producer like him. But what he told me was not what I wanted to hear. He said that I had several paths to producing, but even if I did everything right, I might not get exactly where I wanted.

What?! I won't get an Oscar? I remember my pen flipped out of my hand, and I felt like a toddler having a tantrum. I still feel embarrassed thinking about it now.

But what Barrie wanted me to understand was that the process and enjoying what you do is more important than anything else.

Following your curiosity and doing things you're interested in gives you energy and joy. As a result of pursuing painting, I wrote this book. And I started to feel like I was living the kind of life I only dreamed about before.

If you're still doubting and have no idea what you'd like to try, then finish these sentences:

- If I had more time, I'd love to...
- I have always wanted to...
- If I had enough money and didn't need to worry about taking care of anyone else, I would...
- I so wish I could...
- I feel so much joy when I...
- Wouldn't it be great to try...

Can you see what the common theme is? What do you want to be doing? Remember, it doesn't need to be a money-making activity, and you don't have to know how to make money with what you are interested in doing.

Dig deeper and ask the question: Why do I want this?

It doesn't have to be ground-breaking or world-saving; it could simply be because it brings you joy. And that's a great reason.

CHAPTER FIVE

Creating a Joy List

"The trick is in what one emphasizes. We either make ourselves miserable, or we make ourselves happy. The amount of work is the same."
- Carlos Castaneda

About ten years ago, I gave away my colouring books. They were full of pretty princesses and flowers, and I wanted to colour them in, but I never seemed to find the time. They were tucked away on the shelf, not coloured, so when I moved one more time, I decided to let them go. I figured I was an adult, and colouring books were for kids.

Adult colouring books became popular just a couple of years later. I didn't colour because I thought I had more important things to do. How could I do something I wanted and enjoyed when I hadn't done what needed to be done? I still didn't have a six-figure business.

At the time, a six-figure business was a good deal. Then it quickly became seven-figure, and now there are conversations about eight-figure businesses and multiple eight-figures.

I wondered how I could pause and do something that I enjoyed if I wasn't where social media told me I should be by now. Maybe just like me, you feel like you don't deserve joy if you don't achieve what you want to achieve. Maybe you think that other people need your attention, and you need to help them first.

But you need to remember that when you start doing things that you enjoy, you feel happier, in a flow, more content, and enjoy your life more. You show up differently for yourself and the people around you.

It's a little like exercise. I could talk about how good exercising is for you forever, and you could read about it too, but until you actually start exercising, you will never see the difference. The great thing about doing things you enjoy is that the results are almost immediate. You feel uplifted, energised, and pleased. And those are good feelings to feel, don't you think?

We all want more joy and happiness in our lives. Yet we put most of our effort into the opposite.

Sometimes we even forget what we enjoy entirely. Let's uncover a few things that you enjoy doing and experiencing with a few questions:

- What season do you like the most and why?

- What smells do you like?

- What's your favourite colour?

- What are your favourite flowers?

- What's your favourite meal of the day?

- What do you like to watch and read about?

- What is your favourite kind of music?

- What do you enjoy doing in the morning? During the day? In the evening? Over the weekend?

- What did you enjoy doing when you were a kid? When you were a teenager?

- Imagine you're 80 years old. What did you wish you'd done that you now know would add more joy to your life?

You just started creating your Joy List. Add more things that you enjoy. Think of all the senses and about being, doing, and having. Add things that you think you might enjoy. For me, it's indoor rock climbing, oil painting, and French cooking classes.

Things on your Joy List don't have to be big or elaborate. I enjoy drinking tea from a pretty cup. It's a luxurious and joyful experience for me when I can have tea and do absolutely nothing other than have tea. No movies to watch, no spreadsheets to fill in, and no calls to make. Just a tea. I shall do this more often.

What do you tell yourself that you should do more often, not because it's useful or healthy but just because you like and enjoy doing it?

When I got my heart broken, what helped me out of what seemed like never-ending pain was listening to music. I would lay on my bed with my headphones in and listen to the music I enjoyed. I would only pay attention to what I was listening to, staying in the moment. And in those moments, the heaviness from my heart was lifted, and I could breathe.

I still love doing that, lying on my bed and listening to some music in the middle of the day. Dancing is another thing I know I should do more often. Movement and music can improve your mood very quickly.

In high school, I used to love going through art history books and books filled with various artists' works. I was studying at art school and wanted to be an artist. But when I was about to finish high school, someone told me that I should do something like fashion or interior design because I couldn't be just an artist. There is no money in it.

So, I convinced myself that I wanted to do fashion. And I loved fashion. But I didn't get into fashion or interior design the next year. The competition was ruthless, with only five spots (ten for interior design) open for the whole country. Even with the small Estonia population, it was a huge competition.

I ended up trying to do interior design at a private university before choosing a completely different direction: economics. After that, I suppressed my desire, and I didn't paint for over twenty years. I thought, once I make a certain amount of money, then I'll have time to paint.

The thing is, we don't even have to do everything professionally. We can do things just because we enjoy doing them; writing, painting, sewing, designing. As we talked about in the chapter on the difference between a job, hobby, career, and vocation, we can do our art regardless of what we do for a living.

If you enjoy writing, for example, then start publishing your work on a blog or Medium or another platform. We get better by doing something repeatedly, and it allows us to get feedback from people. I'm not talking about the trolls who do nothing but sit on their couches writing nasty comments but from those who are on a similar journey as you are.

You don't have to have aspirations to be a famous writer, just enjoy the process of writing your thoughts down or starting a blog. Decorate your house with your own pottery or woodwork or paint a few pieces in acrylics. What's important is that you're doing something you enjoy.

If you enjoy walking near the beach, try to do this daily. Is the beach too far away? Listen to the waves on the Tide app while walking around your neighbourhood. You could even have ocean ambience on YouTube while you're making your breakfast – just like that, you're having breakfast at a cafe with an ocean view.

As you learned in the morning ritual chapter, you can create beautiful and enjoyable experiences for yourself. My favourite thing to do is have a candle lit and my tea next to me in a waterfront coffee shop or a cosy bookshop, with a fireplace ambience on my phone (and focus mode on) while I write my morning pages.

I learned about this practice from Julia Cameron. Morning pages are three A4 pages (roughly 750 words) of writing about anything that is on your mind on that particular morning. These pages are not something that you'll publish (however, they often spark ideas for my blogs and newsletters). Instead, it's simply everything that bothers you, that comes to your mind.

After you write for a few weeks and you go back to what you wrote, you may notice some things that you repeat over and over again about what you want to be doing, what you enjoy or what you don't like. It will help you to uncover who you truly are. We'll talk about this more later in the book, and why it's important for your joy.

Julia Cameron also talks about the importance of having artist dates in her book *The Artist's Way*. An artist date is a date with yourself (or your inner artist, if you prefer). These are ideally two hours per week when you do anything you feel like doing. Anything that your inner child, your inner artist, would like to do. Anything that you're curious about. It can be picking leaves and making a collage, trying ikebana or knitting, building a sandcastle, or baking a cake from scratch.

These dates help you to become more joyful and more creative. They help you explore things and understand yourself better. Figure out what you like and don't like that much, what you want to be doing and what you don't want to try again.

Over time, you'll understand who you are better, and getting to know yourself is one of the most important things you can do in life. We'll talk more about this in chapter seven.

Your Turn

Create your Joy List and commit to doing something from your list every day.

CHAPTER SIX

Letting Yourself Rest

*"Yesterday I was clever,
so I wanted to change the world.
Today I am wise, so I am changing myself."*
- Rumi

I woke up in the middle of the night. I wasn't sure what time it was, but I still felt very tired. I looked at my phone, and I still had two hours to sleep. Two more hours felt like a lot when I slept about four to six hours at the time.

I've read many articles about successful people doing all these incredible things while sleeping four hours a night. I wanted to be successful, so I thought I could survive on four hours of sleep while working twelve hours a day and building my online business on the side.

I felt exhausted almost all the time.

I wanted to create a healthier way of making movies (and still do). I tried to come up with systems and wanted to share them, but I realised that a lot of production offices were happier reinventing the wheel every time they started a new production and then complaining about the crazy work hours.

Working an insane number of hours and sacrificing everything was and still is very popular. But there is a new movement that emphasises the importance of rest and sleep and the importance of living your life rather than working your life.

A friend once told me, "Sometimes I look forward to being sick so I can rest." I thought that sounded awful. Yet, I noticed that I, too, didn't allow myself to rest unless I was sick. After teaching Pilates and learning about health and wellness, I knew that if I let myself rest and didn't pressure myself to exercise or do anything I didn't feel like doing, I would recover quickly and return to exercising again sooner.

Why couldn't I allow myself to rest and spend an afternoon with a book when I felt fine? Wouldn't it be more fun to rest without excruciating migraines or a constantly running nose?

There is always something to do, always something to finish, and so little time to pause and rest.

What I've been doing for quite a few years now is getting proper sleep. After some years of little sleep because of work or later insomnia (I learned that I could take off nail polish from my toes while I couldn't sleep – gel nail polish, that was), I now sleep about 8 hours a night. It helps me feel better mentally, physically, and emotionally.

When I don't sleep well, I wake up irritated and annoyed. I can't focus, and I eat more than I normally would just to stay awake. We all understand the importance of rest and sleep, and yet we don't make time for it.

Here is what helped me to sleep better:

- Putting my alarm on in advance so I don't flash the phone light in my face just before I sleep. Ideally, you shouldn't have your phone in your bedroom, but I'm still working on this.

- No work at least two hours before bed. Otherwise, my brain kept working when I was supposed to be going to bed.

- Chamomile tea. It can be a different kind of tea, just the kind that is not stimulating and naturally doesn't have any caffeine.

- If I do wake up during the night, I prefer to get up and have a chamomile tea and read a paper book or journal rather than stay in bed awake. Once I feel sleepy, I go back to bed.

- Sometimes, I take the blanket off to get a bit cold, and once I cover myself up, I'd feel cosy and warm and can fall asleep almost immediately.

- Socks work miracles if you get cold feet.

I believe resting is as essential as sleep. And resting means that you don't do work and don't think of work while you do something for pleasure. When you have time off, read a fiction book, go for a walk, or talk to your partner instead of checking your emails.

Sometimes doing what we enjoy feels like rest, too. It could be painting, walking, reading, cooking, or surfing (even if it doesn't feel like rest physically, it gives you that "mental" rest).

Your Turn

If you can't decide what rest means for you, here are some questions:

- Even if you're unsure, what do you consider rest?

- When do you feel rested?

- What happened before you last felt rested?

- What do you enjoy doing that makes you feel rested, relaxed and re-energised?

- When you feel down, what helps you to get back up?

Refer to this list when you feel anxious and in need of some rest.

CHAPTER SEVEN

Getting to Know Yourself

"You can be the ripest, juiciest peach in the world, and there's still going to be somebody who hates peaches."
- Dita Von Teese

Do you remember that scene from Runaway Bride when Julia Roberts' character prepares all kinds of eggs to figure out what kind she likes for breakfast?

She'd been taking on the interests and tastes of her partners and wasn't herself in the relationships. She didn't know who she was. She felt lost in the relationship and her life, and as a result, she kept running from her weddings.

Knowing yourself will help you in all areas of your life. Most importantly, it will help you to understand what brings you joy and when you feel your best self. Trying to be a chameleon to please everyone around you will leave you feeling irritated, upset, and maybe even angry.

Unfortunately, you may forget who you are if you've been trying to be someone else for a while. It could be scary to be yourself. What if your friends don't like you? What if your partner is disappointed?

You may not have a problem being yourself and don't need this chapter, but if you secretly wonder if you show up as the true you, then keep reading.

I'm still on a journey of figuring out who I am. Being the eldest of three kids, I was always the "grown-up" one, the one who should look after her sister and her brother and put their needs first. Maybe you, as a parent, focus on your kids' needs and forget how to be yourself instead of a mum.

I started by figuring out how I wanted to feel. Danielle La Porte has a whole book on how to figure out your core desired feelings. For me, I want to feel connected, safe, healthy, free, and appreciated, and I want to feel and be surrounded by beauty.

From there, I looked at values. What do you value? What's important for you in your life? They will probably overlap with your desired feelings. My values are enjoyment, connection, beauty, freedom, creativity, ease, and grace.

While looking at what's important, figure out what's non-negotiable. My non-negotiable is trust. When people break my trust, I find it difficult (if ever) to go back to the same relationship with them.

For ideas, Google 'Core Values Lists'. Go over the values and see what resonates with you. Write them all down in the workbook you downloaded. Then, read them again. Do some of them mean almost the same to you? Pick one of them. Or combine two of them. Once you have five or six values, write down what they mean to you. For me, connection means family and friends. Ease and grace mean taking care of my wellness and listening to my intuition.

Look back at your meaning of success from chapter one; this will help you identify what you value. Your Joy List will also help. Knowing what you like is a part of knowing yourself.

When I used to do branding and web design for my clients, I wanted to know not only what they liked but also what they didn't like and why. This way, I could understand what they want better.

You can do a similar exercise for yourself by listing what you don't like. Make sure that after this exercise, you return to your Joy List, re-read it, and add a couple more things, so the positive impact outweighs the negative.

Listen to your inner voice. That kind and curious voice in your head that keeps talking to you, not the monkey voice that critiques and makes fun of you and maybe even says terrible things about you. Listen to the voice that whispers ideas to you: wouldn't it be nice to have an afternoon with a book and a tea? Go for a long walk without your phone? Take a class in art history?

One of the most interesting projects I've done to get to know myself better was creating my manifesto. It's a collection of my values, strengths, what each means to me, my purpose statement, and my vision. I have a vision for my health, lifestyle, relationship, friends & family, purposeful work, and personal growth & spirituality. I made my manifesto into a "presentation" in Canva filled with images that reflect what I've written.

You may want to create something similar for yourself. If you want more information, I highly recommend Erin Tetarenko's leadership courses and coaching (https://www.erintetarenko.com/). Erin's retreats sound fabulous as well and are on my bucket list.

There are some questions in the workbook that will get you started on your manifesto. Give it a go, and you'll discover more about yourself and what matters to you the most.

Getting to know yourself will also help you through difficult times, even though feeling joyful when going through hardship can be tricky. We'll talk about this in the next chapter and what you can do if you're currently in a difficult situation.

CHAPTER EIGHT

Being Joyful During Difficult Times

"If it can be solved, there is no need to worry, and if it can't be solved, worry is of no use."
- Dalai Lama

I was looking forward to my parents and my brother coming over to visit me in Australia for the first time since I moved here. Everything was ready for them, and I was putting final touches on the apartment to make it looks nice for them, when I got a message that after driving 200 km to the airport, they couldn't get on the plane. We didn't apply for the e-visas. I started applying for their visas while they were at the airport waiting, and while my brother's visa came through right away, my parents' visas didn't. They lost the flight.

I blamed myself for not looking into this sooner, assuming that it would be something like a visa on arrival. We lost money on the tickets, and I was infuriated that the people at the airline's check-in desk didn't help my family and wouldn't listen to me after I spoke to the immigration in Australia. I blamed myself for not merging the calls so the person in Tallinn airport could hear the situation for herself.

The visas came through a few hours later, but the plane had already left. I asked my parents to stay in Tallinn instead of travelling home again, but they decided to go home.

The next day, my sister bought another three tickets because she couldn't bear for them not to go. It had been 17 years since I moved to Australia, but nobody from my family had visited me yet, so this was a big event for them and me.

The day they were due to fly, I was sitting in my favourite coffee shop. It was early morning in Estonia, and my family was about to leave home. After a while, I thought my mum should have sent a message by now letting me know they had left because they had two and a half hours to drive. I started to get a bit impatient and nervous.

Then I tried to call my mum, no answer. I called my brother, no answer. Then I got a call from my sister. She told me there had been an accident. I remember seeing myself like I was looking at myself from the outside. What accident? How? My brother has made these trips hundreds of times, and it was early in the morning. How, where? Are they ok? Can they still come?

I finally got in touch with my brother. He was ok; my mum was ok. My dad wasn't. A drunk driver had drifted into the opposite lane and crashed into the car with my parents and my brother inside. And that driver was totally ok.

The emergency services were already there trying to get my dad out. He spent eleven days in the ICU.

The day after the accident, I flew to Estonia. It was the longest flight I had ever taken, but it was the only flight I could get. I was afraid that my dad would die while I was on the plane and feared the same until he was moved out of the ICU.

It was so painful to see him like that. It was so painful to see my mum wearing a neck brace. I was terrified when my brother started getting terrible pain, and we thought the doctors had missed something. Thank God, Universe, and Higher Power they hadn't.

I was so, so sad. And so, so angry. I wrote long emails to the airline telling them what happened because they didn't let my family on the plane, and I demanded a refund for the tickets. They sent me back short responses that it was unfortunate, but there was nothing they could do.

I was glad that my sister was able to get a refund for the tickets she paid for, at least. Even now, writing this, I can't stop crying.

I took a book with me when I flew to Estonia; The Magic by Rhonda Byrne (thanks so much, my dear beautiful Kate, for sending it to me). I needed some magic at the time.

The very first chapter talks about gratitude. I was supposed to compile a list of ten things I was grateful for daily.

My first thought was, seriously? What could I possibly be grateful for right now? Then I realised that I was. I was grateful that my family was ok. I was grateful that my dad went through surgery ok. I was grateful that my brother was ok. I was grateful when my mum could take off the neck brace. I was grateful that I had enough money to buy a ticket and come over. I was grateful that I could have this time with my family. I was grateful that everyone was alive.

Every day, I wrote my list and went through the book. I got myself a tiny "gratitude rock" that I held every evening and would say what I was grateful for, even for the things that hadn't happened yet. I was grateful that my dad would walk by himself again. It did happen. He still uses a cane, but he walks.

That book helped me a lot during that time. Slowly, I let go of the anger at the airline lady who didn't help my family. I even flew that airline recently, and the lady at the check-in was lovely.

My brother did come to see me two years after the accident, and we had a fantastic time. Right on time, just before Covid started.

I truly believe that gratitude helped me through that difficult time and helped me to feel more joyful, even though it was challenging to be joyful.

Back in February 2022, when the chaos started in Ukraine, my niece (my cousin's daughter) decided to escape Kyiv with just a backpack. I couldn't sleep researching how she could get out, and so many people were open to help. In the end, she found her way herself, and all I did was buy a plane ticket and, later, find inexpensive accommodation for her sister with her daughter, who followed her route out of Kyiv. They got to France.

My niece was worried for those who stayed behind, now she was safe, so I sent her a message with words that helped me so many times:

"You can't make yourself sick enough to help the sick. You can't make yourself poor enough to help the poor. You can't make yourself sad enough to help the depressed."

It's up to you if you decide to feel joyful or if you decide to feel sad. But when you choose joy, you can be helpful to those who are in a difficult situation.

Your Turn

- In your journal or your workbook, list ten things you're grateful for today.

- Expand on them – why are you grateful for those things?

- How do you feel after writing about what you are grateful for?

If you are still unsure if you can be joyful in difficult times or find it challenging to be joyful, I hope the next chapter will give you one more tool to help.

CHAPTER NINE

Being Present with Mindfulness

"The past is already gone, the future is not yet here. There's only one moment for you to live, and that is the present moment."
- Buddha

Some time ago, I found myself sitting and waiting to see a psychologist for the first time. Thoughts raced through my head, "I could not possibly see a psychologist. I'm not crazy. Only crazy people need a psychologist. I should leave."

But I didn't. I was in such a deep black hole, and I couldn't find a reason why I was in this world; I was in the wrong relationship, trying to get a job and getting dozens of refusals, trying to get my online business up and running for the wrong reasons. I cried several times a day, not knowing how I could escape that feeling of helplessness and sorrow.

I remember looking down the balcony in the shopping centre and thinking, what if I could just fly? I would never do it, of course, and I cried thinking about what it would do to my mum and my family.

I needed help. When I went to see my doctor and explained that I cry almost all the time (while I cried sitting opposite her), she asked me to fill in a questionnaire. I got a lot of points, and that meant I needed a psychologist.

That very first psychologist introduced me to mindfulness. I don't claim that it's the depression cure, but after listening to various talks and learning more about depression, I found out more about mindfulness and simple exercises I could do.

It was strange at first to focus on something I was doing in the moment. I would go through my day without really thinking about it. So, paying full attention to what I was doing in the moment sounded highly audacious.

I decided to do my first mindfulness exercise with tea. I always loved tea and going to a pretty restaurant with a view of my favourite building in Sydney—the Queen's Victoria Building—was a treat. The waiter brought me tea with a cup, and I poured the tea through the little sieve. It was hot.

The cup was white. I looked at the building through the window, and I was happy in that moment. Delicious tea and a beautiful view. The tea tasted terrific. I'm unsure if the tea was that excellent or if my attention made it so, but I was happy. Nothing else existed at that moment.

Another practice I love and still do daily is paying attention to all my senses. You can do this practice sitting, standing, or lying down:

- First, look around yourself and name (out loud or in your mind) five things around you: yellow flowers, green leaves, brown deck, blue sky, red pencil.

- Then close your eyes and name four sounds: birds chirping, the dishwasher whirling, the wind, your breath.

- Next, pay attention to your breath. Inhale and exhale. Focus on three of your breaths. It's like you weren't breathing before, right?

- Next is feeling. Name two or three feelings; I prefer to do three. The pressure on your bones sitting on the carpet, your top against your skin, the wind blowing on your face.

- Finally, swallow once and pay attention. What do you taste?

The full combination is 5-4-3-2-1. But you can do three of each sense or try different combinations if you prefer (I can never taste more than one thing, so I always stick to one for the last one). I then take a few minutes to sit with my eyes closed and meditate after this mindfulness exercise.

These practices seem so simple, and you might wonder if they make any difference. But they do make a difference. As with everything else, it doesn't need to be complicated to get results.

Being present is where you find joy. If you think about the past, you get stuck in regret, shame, or disappointment. If you're too much in the future, you feel anxiety or fear. But if you focus on your breathing, on what's happening right this moment, there is no danger, there is no disappointment or regret, only now.

If you do feel that you need a specialist, talk with your doctor. If one doctor doesn't help, go see another.

Mental health is important because it affects how we feel and our overall physical health. So, next, let's talk about how physical health contributes to our joy.

CHAPTER TEN

Taking Care of Your Physical Health

"Exercise is the key not only to physical health but to peace of mind."
- Nelson Mandela

Do you like being pushed and pressured? I doubt it. But how often do you push and pressure yourself? To get more done because it's all about being productive, to complete projects because you started them, to not let yourself rest because how could you rest if you haven't done what you were meant to do?

We often tell ourselves the ugliest things that we would never tell our friends or even people we don't like much, and yet we criticise ourselves, our bodies, and our results and diminish our achievements.

There are parts of us that we like and parts we don't. But we forget the good parts and tend to focus on the bad parts. But imagine that all the parts of you are girls (or boys) sitting on a bus together. If someone is unwell or upset, everyone helps them because you need all these girls to continue travelling. They are parts of you.

A considerable percentage of people are unhappy with their bodies for at least one stage in their life. For many, it's a constant struggle and the "I need to lose weight" mantra rings in their head from the morning until the evening.

When I used to teach Pilates, I often told people that when you start loving your body the way it is now and start exercising because you care about your body and not because you need to lose weight, you'll start getting results beyond your expectations. It's magic, but it's true.

You don't have to exercise for hours to see results, starting with just ten minutes of stretching, yoga or some Pilates movements. This will also build a habit of exercising, and then gradually, you can increase the length of your workouts.

I always taught pelvic floor exercises as a Pilates instructor. Pelvic floor muscles are often overlooked, and not a lot of people know about them. But they are probably the most important muscles in your body, followed by the transverse abdominis muscles – the deepest of the abdominal muscles. The stronger you are in your pelvic floor and transverse abdominis, the better your posture is, the flatter your stomach is, the less pressure you feel on your lower back, and the more difficult exercises you can attempt without injuring yourself.

If you would like to learn more about how to activate and strengthen your pelvic floor muscles, check the secret page on my website: https://www.olyakornienko.com/t-zone-secret

The physical movement not only helps your body stay in shape, but it also helps your mood. Have you ever dragged yourself to a yoga class and then been so grateful that you did it? You might have even felt on top of the world, it felt so good. It may be a run, a HIIT workout, or a studio Pilates session. Try to find something that you like. Dancing is a great way to exercise as well.

What we tell ourselves in our minds is even more important than the physical movement. Until I figured that out, I was always on the "lose more weight" journey. I'm not saying that you can just think yourself thin and healthy without exercising or eating healthy but helping yourself through positive thinking and kindness towards yourself and your body will make everything so much easier.

The water experiment by Japanese scientist Masaru Emoto demonstrates this beautifully. Water is divided into two glasses. One glass of water is exposed to all the good stuff: beautiful music, words, and images. It's told how beautiful and marvellous it is. The other glass of water is exposed to ugly, negative words. Then, the water is frozen and examined under a microscope.

The water that experienced love crystallised into the most beautiful shapes, whereas water that experienced hatred did not have any shape at all.

Our bodies are 60% water. So, when you tell yourself unkind words about your body, you literally make it shapeless. Start telling yourself kind words, and you'll notice small changes. Even if your body is not exactly the way you want it to be right now, find something beautiful about your body. Tell yourself wonderful words that you would say to someone you love dearly.

You've heard this before, but if the oxygen mask drops on the plane, you must put that mask on yourself before helping someone else. You must take good care of yourself, so you can take care of others.

This comes back to doing things you enjoy. When you allow yourself to do and experience things you enjoy, everything else falls into place. You feel more joyful and more energetic, you're happier, and you'll take better care of yourself.

There is no best place to start, and there is no end. Everything is interconnected, and it is a journey. You can start with anything you want. Maybe for you, that's practising gratitude. Or creating your morning ritual. No matter what you choose or where you begin, you'll add more joy to your life. And if you follow this book, in whatever order you choose, you'll add more joy to your life. The order doesn't matter because every step and every moment counts.

CONCLUSION

A Letter to The Reader

"You can fail at what you don't want, so you might as well take a chance on doing what you love."
- Jim Carrey

My dear reader,

In case you forgot, here is your reminder: You are an artist.

You don't want to be an artist? Fine. Enjoying life doesn't need to be artistic if you don't want it to be. But it can be enjoyable, and there is no need for sacrifice. There is no need to be tough and push through.

You can just move forward. You can choose joy. You can pause and do things you love. You don't have to be perfect, you don't have to have a multiple eight-figure business, your own TV show, and your face on the cover of a magazine. You don't have to have a villa in Bali or a mansion in California. You can be joyful now, today, this week.

You can choose joy. You can do things you love. Trying to do it all and be everything for everyone else will distort your strength, damage your health, and demolish your mental wellbeing.

Please be gentle with yourself. It's a journey. There is no immediate result. It's like brushing your teeth. You do that every day, rarely with an expectation that it will get you a fabulous Hollywood smile. But in the end, it does you good.

You have a choice: keep doing what you've always done or choose joy. Deliberately choose to do things purely because they feel good. Because they feel light.

Is it easy? It can be. Society tells us that life is difficult; you can't achieve success without sacrifice, hard work, pushing, and neglecting your desire to rest. But what if you choose ease and grace? If you choose joy and the things that make you feel warm and cosy, like a cup of tea or a glass of red?

Please remember, it won't be perfect. You'll probably stuff it up. And even if you do everything right, you may still not get where you want to be. What can go wrong will go wrong. But there is a chance that, in the end, it will turn out to be fabulous. And if it's not, you've done things and had experiences that you enjoyed.

What could be better than that?

With love and gratitude,

Olya

Acknowledgements

I have wanted to write a book for a long time, and it does take a village to write a book. So, a huge thank you to…

My mum, for always allowing me to try and pursue things I'm interested in.

My family, the kindest and most supportive family in the world. I'm so lucky to have you.

My partner, who always believes in hard work. I love you for this and many other reasons, even though I do believe that life should be easy.

My dear Dominique, who always supported me with her (often tough) love and who taught me a lot about copywriting, work ethics, and focusing on the task at hand. I miss you so much.

Barrie Osborne, for the best advice I ever received, even though I didn't understand it when I got it, and for your support.

Elisa, Ian, John, Josh, and Michael, you helped me to believe that the impossible is possible.

Elena Kozliakova, my dear friend, for listening to all my worries and whining, celebrating my wins, and constantly reminding me that what I've achieved so far is quite a big deal.

Jane, for our tea catch-ups and the artists' journey together (even if we didn't finish it).

Oksana Belo, for our friendship, our "podcasts", and shared love of beauty.

Kate Forsatz, for our friendship and shared love of movies.

Ivana Dirlic, for our conversations and educating me on body psychotherapy.

Stephanie King, for your often uncomfortable questions that gave me the strength to do things I thought I couldn't and for teaching me how to say no.

The Tiny Book Course founders, Alexandra Franzen (I followed you for so long and I finally wrote my book!) and Lindsay Smith.

Tiny Book coaches Kayla and Tracie. You're amazing!

Emily Williams, for the brilliant edit of this book and so many articles. I don't know what I would have done without you.

Pia Edberg, my first book coach, thank you for giving me the foundation to start writing a book.

Ivelina, for this beautiful book cover and workbook

Dani Batista, thanks so much for your friendship and all the work we've done together.

Carolina, a huge thank you for your support, kindness and encouragement.

Erin Tetarenko, for helping me to discover my vision and my strengths, creating my manifesto.

Victoria Carwin, my friend and talented producer and a believer that we can make it.

Frieda Levycky, for the inspiration, amazing value discovery exercise, friendship, and support.

Michelle Simmonds, who was the first one back in 2014 who I told that I wanted to write a book and who has supported me ever since. Michelle, I wish I had listened to you sooner!

Katie Wood, who helped me to finally start painting again after twenty years.

Katherine North, thank you for your extraordinary newsletters and the inspiration to be different and to finally write and publish my book.

Julie Van den Kerchove, who's wise beyond her years, spiritual and supportive, and an amazing chef and author of so many books (that also helped me to believe I could do it, too).

Nadezhda Nikolaevna, my literature teacher, for teaching me how to write in high school, even if we disagree on Lolita and Pour People.

Anette Meberg, a very talented and wonderful young lady. Thank you for the beautiful photo that you took of me that I used for the back cover.

Anna, Sonata, Meg, Jessica, Anabel, Laura, Berit, and Gulnara, thank you for your friendship and support.

Everyone who inspires me every day: Marie Forleo, Gabrielle Bernstein, Elizabeth Gilbert, Seth Godin, Steven Pressfield, Fiona Ferris, Jen Sincero, Nancy Levin, Denise Duffield-Thomas, Pilar Alessandra, Jessica Rose Williams, Cheryl Strayed, Michelle Obama, Austin Kleon, James Wedmore, Louise Hay, Adele and, of course, Oprah.

Approximately one million other people that I am forgetting right now.

Thank you. Everyone.

Book Bonuses

I wanted you to get the most out of this book, and created these bonuses with you in mind:

- Your own editable workbook filled with questions and space to write down your answers.

- A mini-video lesson on how to add more balance and self-care to your life.

- The Add More Balance to Your Life checklist to make sure you're on the right track.

- A subscription to the Inner Circle, where you'll receive personal updates, tools, and advice from me that I only share with my subscribers.

Visit this page to receive your special bonuses:

https://www.olyakornienko.com/a-tiny-book-of-joy-bonuses

A Note from the Author

It was a pleasure to write this book, and I hope you enjoyed reading it. I hope that this tiny book helped you to believe that joy is available now and that it inspired you to try some of the things that you learned from it.

When you have a moment, I would be so grateful if you could write a review on Amazon. These reviews will help other readers who want to feel more joy in their lives to find this book.

Thank you for reading my book. If you want to send me an email and share what you liked the most about it or share your own tip, you can send it to: olya@olyakornienko.com.

Take good care of yourself,

Olya

About the Author

Olya Kornienko is an author who specialises in joy, creativity, and wellness. She's worked in the film and TV, accounting, fashion, and wellness industries for over two decades.

From sewing samples for the most exclusive lingerie line in Australia to teaching Pilates to thousands of people online and offline, Olya certainly has a variety of experiences. She has over 2.5 million views on her YouTube channel, produced a short film, and worked on the Great Gatsby, Underbelly and Getaway.

Olya grew up in Estonia but is based in Sydney, Australia. She loves being with her family, painting, yoga, walking, the ocean, art, watching rom-coms and movies based on true stories, the show "Friends", and travelling (and so much more).

This is her first book, and hopefully not her last.

To learn more about Olya, visit her website: http://www.olyakornienko.com/

Reading List

Steal Like an Artist by Austin Kleon (chapter 2)
Video: Elizabeth Gilbert on *Distinguishing Between Hobbies, Jobs, Careers, Vocation* - Acumen Academy (chapter 2)
Everything is Figureoutable by Marie Forleo (chapter 4)
You Are a Badass at Making Money: Master the Mindset of Wealth by Jen Sincero (chapter 4)
Video: Mel Robbins - *Don't Know What You Want? Answer This Question* (chapter 4)
The Artist's Way by Julia Cameron (chapter 5)
Erin Tetarenko's website: https://erintetarenko.com (chapter 7)
The Desire Map: A Guide to Creating Goals with Soul by Danielle LaPorte (chapter 7)
The Magic by Rhonda Byrne (chapter 8)
Video: Water experiment by Japanese scientist Maseru Emoto (chapter 10)
Secret page to learn about the T-zone: https://www.olyakornienko.com/t-zone-secret (chapter 10)

Notes

www.ingramcontent.com/pod-product-compliance
Lightning Source LLC
Chambersburg PA
CBHW010707020526
44107CB00082B/2708